STR
NONPROFITS

Empowering Change through Monitoring and Evaluation

OLASHENI SOMOTUN

CONTENTS

FOREWORD

Welcome to the comprehensive guide "Strategic Nonprofits: Empowering Change through Monitoring & Evaluation." In today's dynamic world, the effective management and evaluation of nonprofit programs have taken on heightened significance. Faced with limited resources and an urgent need for impactful change, nonprofits are tasked with ensuring their efforts are both strategic and accountable. Monitoring and evaluation offer the essential tools and frameworks to achieve these crucial goals.

This guide takes you on an illuminating journey through the fundamental concepts, methodologies, and best practices of monitoring and evaluation within the nonprofit sector. Across its diverse chapters, you will gain a robust understanding of the core principles of monitoring and evaluation, accompanied by pragmatic advice on designing, implementing, and harnessing monitoring and evaluation plans.

Chapter 1 lays the foundation by introducing monitoring and evaluation's pivotal role, defining their importance, and exploring their significance in nonprofit management. This chapter primes your understanding, establishing the value and purpose of monitoring and evaluation within nonprofit organizations.

Chapter 2 dives into the process of crafting a monitoring and evaluation plan. It maps out the essential steps, spanning from setting goals and objectives to pinpointing data requirements, choosing suitable data collection methods, analysing data, and reporting findings. This comprehensive guide equips nonprofit leaders and practitioners with a robust framework for building effective monitoring and evaluation systems.

Chapter 3 shines the spotlight on implementing a monitoring and evaluation plan. It delves into the practical aspects of data collection, analysis, and reporting findings. Moreover, it underscores the pivotal role findings play in elevating nonprofit programs and fostering evidence-based decision-making for program enhancements.

Chapter 4 takes on the challenges often encountered in monitoring and evaluation endeavours. It tackles issues like resource constraints, time limitations, skill gaps, and organizational commitment. Acknowledging and comprehending these challenges empowers nonprofit leaders to devise strategies that surmount obstacles, ensuring the successful execution of monitoring and evaluation initiatives.

Chapter 5 shifts focus to strategies for overcoming the challenges discussed in the previous chapter. Enhancing internal capabilities, collaborating with external partners, leveraging technology, and embracing flexibility emerge as key strategies to heighten the impact of monitoring and evaluation endeavours.

Chapter 6 shifts the narrative towards using monitoring and evaluation as a catalyst for program improvement. It underscores the importance of tracking progress, identifying areas ripe for enhancement, executing necessary changes, and gauging impact. Real-world illustrations and case studies illuminate the practical application of monitoring and evaluation in propelling programmatic advancements.

Chapter 7 accentuates the role of monitoring and evaluation in bolstering nonprofit accountability. It unearths how monitoring and evaluation findings can exhibit impact, foster stakeholder trust, and attract funding. This chapter unveils the essential connection between accountability and the triumphant operations of nonprofits.

In Chapter 8, we conclude by reiterating the significance of "Empowering Change through Strategic Nonprofits: A Focus on Monitoring & Evaluation." This chapter underscores that monitoring and evaluation are not merely tools but strategic investments yielding lasting benefits. Through ongoing evaluation and enhancement of programs, nonprofits can magnify their influence and uphold their commitment to stakeholders.

Chapter 9 beckons nonprofit leaders to embark on their monitoring and evaluation journey today. It offers insights into available resources, encompassing books, articles, online courses, and professionals ready to extend guidance and support in devising and executing monitoring and evaluation plans.

I warmly invite you to traverse the pages of this guide with an open mind and a readiness to embrace the potency of monitoring and evaluation. By doing so, you equip yourself with knowledge and tools to elevate your nonprofit's effectiveness, impact, and accountability. Together, we are catalysts for positive change, contributing to a brighter world.

Best regards,

Olasheni Somotun MPH.

DEDICATION

To my cherished family, whose unwavering strength and support have been my guiding light. To my loyal friends, who've stood by me through every twist and turn. And to all the visionaries, optimists, and achievers who continually fuel my drive to become the finest iteration of myself.

This book is wholeheartedly dedicated to all of you. May its pages fill your hearts with joy, ignite the flame of hope within you, and embolden you to relentlessly pursue your aspirations. Let it serve as a constant reminder that with self-belief and unwavering perseverance, every goal is within your grasp.

With heartfelt affection and boundless appreciation,

Olasheni Somotun MPH.

CHAPTER 1:

An Introduction to Monitoring and Evaluation

Nonprofit organizations play a crucial role in addressing societal challenges encompassing social, environmental, and economic issues (Smith, 2020). However, assessing the efficacy of nonprofit programs and initiatives poses a challenge due to their intricate and ever-changing nature.

Enter the realm of monitoring and evaluation (M&E). M&E is a methodical and unbiased process involving data collection, analysis, and utilization to monitor progress and gauge the impact of programs and initiatives over time (Bamberger, Rao, & Woolcock, 2010).

Numerous reasons underscore the importance of M&E for nonprofits. Firstly, it enables organizations to appraise the achievement of intended outcomes and objectives within their programs. This data is indispensable for well-informed decisions regarding program design, resource allocation, and strategic planning (Patton, 2011).

Secondly, M&E offers concrete evidence of program effectiveness, serving as a foundation for engaging stakeholders like funders, beneficiaries, and policymakers.

This empirical backing is pivotal for sustaining support and funding for nonprofit initiatives (Ebrahim & Rangan, 2010). Lastly, M&E facilitates the growth and enhancement of nonprofits by identifying areas for betterment and avenues for innovation (Chen & Fang, 2015).

Process monitoring and impact evaluation emerge as the two main branches of M&E (Bamberger et al., 2010). Process monitoring revolves around overseeing program and activity execution, encompassing service delivery and resource utilization.

This facet of M&E aids in pinpointing challenges during program implementation and furnishes insights for program enhancement. Conversely, impact evaluation scrutinizes program effectiveness in achieving stipulated outcomes and impacts.

This form of M&E proves indispensable in understanding the cause-and-effect relationship between programs and outcomes and ascertaining the desired impact.

M&E serves a multifaceted role in nonprofit management. Primarily, it guarantees accountability and transparency by substantiating program outcomes and impact (Ebrahim & Rangan, 2010).

This holds particular significance for nonprofits reliant on stakeholder trust and backing for operational success. Moreover, M&E informs decision-making by supplying timely, precise information about program performance and impact (Chen & Fang, 2015).

This information aids in real-time program adjustments, responding to emerging challenges, and identifying opportunities for scaling up successful endeavours.

Ultimately, M&E nurtures a culture of learning and improvement within nonprofit organizations, fostering introspection, adaptation, and innovation (Patton, 2011).

In summation, M&E stands as an indispensable instrument for nonprofits in quantifying the efficacy of their programs and initiatives.

By delivering systematic, impartial evidence of program outcomes and impact, M&E empowers organizations to make sound decisions, secure continuous support, and evolve through learning and enhancement.

In the forthcoming chapters, we will delve into the fundamental principles, methodologies, and tools of M&E for nonprofits, offering pragmatic guidance on designing and implementing effective M&E systems.

References

- Bamberger, M., Rao, V., & Woolcock, M. (2010). Using mixed methods in monitoring and evaluation: experiences from International Development. World Bank Publications.
- Chen, H. T., & Fang, C. C. (2015). Understanding nonprofit effectiveness: Applying theories, methods, and metrics. Springer.
- Ebrahim, A., & Rangan, V. K. (2010). The limits of nonprofit impact: A contingency framework for measuring social performance. Harvard Business School Working Paper, (11-099).
- Patton, M. Q. (2011). Developmental evaluation: Applying complexity concepts to enhance innovation and use. Guilford Press.

CHAPTER 2:

Designing a Monitoring and Evaluation Plan

I n the realm of nonprofit organizations, establishing clear goals and objectives is paramount, coupled with a robust system for monitoring and evaluating progress.

This chapter delves into the significance of monitoring and evaluation (M&E) as a process for collecting and analysing data to assess the impact of programs or interventions, ultimately enabling nonprofits to enhance effectiveness, allocate resources wisely, and uphold accountability.

✓ Setting Clear Goals And Objectives

(The initial stride in crafting an M&E plan involves the formulation of distinct goals and objectives.) Goals encapsulate the broad aims of the organization, while objectives are precise, quantifiable targets to be achieved. For instance, in the case of a nonprofit addressing homelessness, a goal might be to end homelessness within a community, with specific objectives like reducing rough sleeping by 50% within two years.

- *Ensuring SMART Goals and Objectives*
  - Specific, measurable, achievable, relevant,

and time-bound goals and objectives guarantee a robust M&E plan.
- Each objective must be well-defined, trackable, achievable within available resources, aligned with the organization's goal, and equipped with a specific deadline.

Identifying Data Requirements

After establishing goals and objectives, the next stride is identifying the requisite data for monitoring and evaluating progress. This entails defining the data to be collected, the frequency of collection, and the responsible parties.

- *Classifying Data Needs*
  - Distinguishing between output and outcome data is pivotal. Output data pertains to program activities, e.g., meals served, or training attendance. Outcome data reflects changes caused by these activities, like increased stable housing due to the organization's efforts.

- *Linking Data Needs to Objectives*
  - Start by scrutinizing objectives to deduce required data, encompassing demographics, services rendered, people served, and outcomes achieved.

Selecting Effective Data Collection Approaches

With data needs identified, the subsequent step is selecting fitting data collection methods. Multiple avenues, such as surveys, interviews, focus groups, observations, and document analysis, cater to various data collection requirements.

- *Tailoring Data Collection Methods*
  - The choice of method hinges on data

needs and resource availability. Surveys are expansive, interviews offer in-depth insights, observations reveal behaviours, and document analysis mines existing records.

- *Considerations in Method Selection*
  - Factors such as cost, time, detail, and potential bias impact method selection.

✓ Analysing Data For Insightful Conclusions

Once data collection is complete, analysis ensues, unearthing insights into progress towards organizational goals. Data analysis, be it quantitative or qualitative, illuminates patterns and trends that shape program efficacy.

- *Quantitative and Qualitative Analysis*
  - Quantitative analysis leverages statistical tools for numerical data, while qualitative analysis deciphers non-numerical data through methods like thematic analysis.

- *Informed Decision-Making*
  - Interpreting data in the context of original intentions and goals aids decision-making, offering valuable insights for program enhancement or innovation.

✓ Presenting Results Effectively

Following data analysis, clear and concise reporting is key. The report should comprise an executive summary, methodological details, and limitations, all tailored for diverse stakeholders' comprehension.

- *Transparent and Accessible Reporting*
  - Employ accessible language, simplifying technical terms for readers unfamiliar with

the field. Visual aids like graphs and charts enhance engagement and clarity.

- *Wider Dissemination of Findings*
  - Consider disseminating findings via diverse channels like presentations, social media, and academic publications to foster learning, collaboration, and program efficacy.

Navigating Limitations And Challenges

Though invaluable, monitoring and evaluation come with limitations and challenges that nonprofits must acknowledge.

- *Common Limitations*
  - Data collection demands time and resources.
  - Data might bear biases or inaccuracies.

- *Frequent Challenges*
  - Scarce resources and staff expertise.
  - Management's commitment to M&E.

Despite these obstacles, embracing monitoring and evaluation empowers nonprofits to elevate effectiveness, resource allocation, and accountability. With careful planning and implementation, nonprofits navigate these challenges to create enduring impact and drive positive change.

CHAPTER 3:

Implementing a Monitoring and Evaluation Plan

After exploring the design phase in Chapter 2, we now delve into the pivotal realm of implementation in Chapter 3. Executing a monitoring and evaluation (M&E) plan involves a seamless flow of data collection, analysis, reporting, and utilization, all aimed at program enhancement and informed decision-making.

This chapter serves as a comprehensive guide to effectively implement M&E plans within the nonprofit sector.

✓ Data Collection: Building The Foundation

Collecting accurate and pertinent data forms the bedrock of any robust M&E plan. Data alignment with set goals is essential. The chapter breaks down the key steps in data collection:

1. *Selecting Data Collection Methods*:
   - Choose suitable methods such as surveys,

interviews, observations, focus groups, or document analysis.
  - Tailor methods based on objectives, target audience, resources, and time constraints.

2. *Developing Data Collection Tools*:
  - Design clear, concise tools like questionnaires, interview guides, or observation checklists.
  - Ensure tools align with M&E plan objectives and test them through pilot runs.

3. *Establishing Data Collection Procedures*:
  - Set clear procedures, train data collectors, establish protocols, and adhere to timelines.
  - Standardize processes to enhance data reliability and comparability.

  .

4. *Executing Data Collection*:
  - With tools and protocols in place, commence data collection while ensuring adherence to established procedures.
  - Regular monitoring and supervision mitigate potential issues during collection.

Analysing Data: Illuminating Insights

The analytical phase holds great significance, transforming collected data into meaningful insights. This chapter outlines key steps in data analysis:

1. *Data Cleaning and Preparation*:

- Prepare data by addressing missing or erroneous data, ensuring accuracy and integrity.

2. *Selecting Analytical Techniques*:
   - Choose appropriate techniques based on data nature and research questions.
   - Quantitative analysis may involve descriptive and inferential statistics, regression, or correlation. Qualitative analysis may identify patterns, themes, or categories.

3. *Conducting Data Analysis*:
   - Apply selected techniques to data, whether through statistical tests, charts, graphs, or qualitative coding.
   - Interpret results objectively, drawing conclusions supported by data.

4. *Validating and Interpreting Results*:
   - Scrutinize analysis process and findings for robustness and bias.
   - Relate results back to M&E plan objectives, ensuring meaningful conclusions.

✓ Reporting Insights: Building Transparency

Clear and comprehensive reporting is vital to accountability, transparency, and organizational learning. The chapter elucidates key components of an effective report:

1. *Executive Summary*:
   - Begin with a concise executive summary capturing key findings, conclusions, and

recommendations.
- Provide a snapshot of M&E outcomes to engage readers.

2. *Methodology*:
- Detail methodology encompassing data collection, sampling, analytical techniques, and limitations.
- Transparent methodology enhances report credibility.

3. *Findings and Analysis*:
- Present findings logically, utilizing tables, charts, or graphs for clarity.
- Analyse results objectively, highlighting key patterns and trends.

4. *Conclusions and Recommendations*:
- Draw evidence-backed conclusions aligned with M&E plan objectives.
- Offer actionable recommendations for program improvement and decision-making.

✓ Leveraging Findings For Impact: Turning Insight Into Action

Utilizing M&E findings is pivotal for driving program enhancement. This chapter outlines steps for utilizing insights:

1. *Reflection and Learning*:
- Engage stakeholders in reflective processes

to collectively analyse findings.
- Create an inclusive environment fostering learning and insight-sharing.

2. *Program Adaptation and Innovation*:
- Utilize findings to adapt and innovate programs based on conclusions and recommendations.
- Identify areas for change and reallocate resources strategically.

3. *Continuous Monitoring and Evaluation*:
- Implement iterative monitoring and evaluation to track program improvements.
- Make ongoing adjustments based on evolving insights.

As the M&E journey unfolds, remember it's a dynamic, iterative process. By effectively executing the steps elucidated in this chapter, nonprofit organizations can seamlessly implement their M&E plans. This leads to well-informed decision-making, elevated program outcomes, and, ultimately, a more significant impact within communities.

CHAPTER 4:

Challenges of Monitoring and Evaluation

Welcome to the insightful journey of Chapter 4 in our comprehensive book, "Strategic Nonprofits: Empowering Change through Monitoring & Evaluation." This chapter serves as a beacon of knowledge, guiding you through the common challenges encountered by nonprofit organizations in the realm of monitoring and evaluation (M&E).

The landscape of M&E is intricate, with its share of hurdles that, once understood and addressed, can pave the way for refined practices and enhanced impact.

So, let's embark on a voyage to explore the four key challenges that nonprofits often grapple with: Lack of Resources, Lack of Time, Lack of Expertise, and Lack of Commitment.

1. Lack Of Resources: Unravelling The Financial Struggle

The first challenge that often looms over nonprofits is the scarcity of resources. In a world where financial, human, and technological resources are coveted, limited access can impede the establishment of robust M&E systems.

Digging Deeper:

i. Financial Constraints: Nonprofits are known to navigate with limited budgets, making it arduous to invest significantly in comprehensive M&E endeavours. Procuring essential software, tools, and external expertise might be constrained by budget limitations.

ii. Human Resources: The absence of dedicated and trained staff members exclusively for M&E can hinder processes like data collection, analysis, and reporting. Challenges arise in balancing available personnel against the demands of comprehensive M&E.

iii. Technological Infrastructure: Insufficient technological infrastructure poses another barrier. Outdated or limited access to computers, software, and reliable internet connectivity can hamper seamless data management, analysis, and reporting.

2. Lack Of Time: Navigating Time's Precious Conundrum

The second challenge unfurls as nonprofits grapple with time constraints. The multitude of concurrent projects and commitments leaves nonprofits with little time to dedicate to thorough M&E practices.

Deconstructing the Issue:

i. Multifaceted Responsibilities: Nonprofit staff members often juggle various responsibilities beyond M&E, such as program implementation, fundraising, stakeholder engagement, and administrative tasks. These simultaneous commitments can limit the time available for meticulous M&E efforts.

ii. Time-Intensive Data Collection: The process of data collection, especially when diverse data sources, methods, or sizable sample sizes are involved, consumes significant time. This tightrope walk between numerous tasks and data collection can prove challenging.

iii. Reporting Deadlines: The looming spectre of deadlines —imposed by funders, grant stipulations, or regulatory bodies—can exert undue pressure. The rush to meet these deadlines might compromise the quality of data analysis and reporting.

3. Lack Of Expertise: Navigating The Knowledge Abyss

Nonprofit organizations often grapple with a scarcity of expertise in the domain of M&E. This challenge is marked by limited knowledge and skills, impacting data collection, analysis, and reporting quality.

Diving into the Issue:

i. Limited Training Opportunities: Access to training programs that can enhance M&E skills might be inadequate for nonprofits. The absence of continuous learning avenues can create a knowledge gap, thwarting the execution of robust M&E practices.

ii. Complex Methodologies: M&E methodologies can be intricate, necessitating specialised knowledge. Nonprofits without proficient staff or external support may find it arduous to adopt suitable methodologies, leading to incomplete or inaccurate data analysis.

iii. Data Interpretation and Utilization: Making informed decisions based on M&E findings requires analytical prowess. Nonprofits lacking expertise in data interpretation might find it challenging to derive actionable insights from evaluation results.

4. Lack Of Commitment: Stepping Up Organizational Involvement

The final challenge deals with organizational commitment to M&E. Without firm backing, M&E might be relegated to an afterthought rather than an integral part of program management.

Peering Closer:

> **i. Perception of Evaluation as Burdensome:** M&E can sometimes be perceived as an administrative burden rather than a tool for learning and growth. This perception might discourage resource allocation and prioritisation of M&E efforts.

> **ii. Resistance to Change:** Organizational culture and a resistance to change can hinder the acceptance of M&E practices. A preference for maintaining the status quo can act as an obstacle to M&E adoption.

> **iii. Lack of Leadership Support:** Strong leadership backing is vital for M&E success. In the absence of leadership endorsement, resource allocation, and integration into the organizational culture, M&E efforts might struggle to take root.

In this chapter, we navigated the rocky terrain of challenges that nonprofit organizations frequently face in the realm of M&E. The dearth of resources, time constraints, limited expertise, and wavering commitment can all pose formidable obstacles.

However, these challenges aren't insurmountable. With strategic planning, resource allocation, capacity building, and wholehearted organizational buy-in, nonprofits can transcend these challenges. By doing so, they elevate their M&E practices, ensuring refined program outcomes and heightened accountability, further fuelling their journey of empowering change.

CHAPTER 5:

Overcoming the Challenges of Monitoring and Evaluation

As we open the doors to Chapter 5 in our comprehensive book, "Strategic Nonprofits: Empowering Change through Monitoring & Evaluation," we embark on a journey of discovery. This chapter delves into an array of dynamic strategies and innovative approaches aimed at overcoming the challenges that nonprofit organizations often encounter during monitoring and evaluation (M&E).

Challenges are an inherent part of this terrain, yet armed with strategic wisdom, nonprofits can transcend these obstacles, harnessing their potential for growth. So, let's navigate through the strategic compass, illuminating pathways to building capacity, forging partnerships, embracing technology, and cultivating flexibility.

1. Building Capacity: Fortifying The Foundation

The first beacon on our strategic map is "Building Capacity." A sturdy internal foundation is indispensable for nonprofits to address M&E challenges effectively. By nurturing knowledge, honing skills, and augmenting resources, organizations empower themselves to establish robust M&E practices.

Diving Deeper:

a) Training and Professional Development:

Fostering a culture of continuous learning through avenues like workshops, seminars, online courses, and conferences bolsters staff expertise. These platforms cater to research methods, data analysis, evaluation frameworks, and result-based management, cultivating a cadre of adept M&E practitioners.

b) Hiring or Engaging Monitoring and Evaluation Experts:

By enlisting the support of experts or collaborating with external consultants, nonprofits tap into specialised knowledge. These adept individuals provide the compass to navigate complex M&E terrains, ensuring precision and rigor.

c) Establishing Monitoring and Evaluation Units:

The creation of dedicated units or teams centred around M&E enhances internal capacity. These units serve as hubs of streamlined processes, standardised methodologies, and a culture imbued with the thirst for learning and growth.

2. Partnering With Others: The Power Of Collective Endeavour

Our second strategic vista shines the spotlight on "Partnering with Others." Collaboration and alliances emerge as potent tools to conquer M&E challenges. By enlisting the support of external stakeholders, nonprofits amplify their impact through shared expertise, resources, and perspectives.

Exploring Further:

a) Collaborating with Academic Institutions:

The synergy with universities, research institutions, and academic luminaries opens doors to research methodologies, data analysis techniques, and evaluation frameworks. This alliance elevates the depth and credibility of M&E endeavours, marking them with academic rigour.

b) Engaging with Peer Organizations:

When nonprofits join hands with kindred spirits sharing similar objectives, they unlock a treasure trove of best practices and collective wisdom. Through collaborative evaluations and experience-sharing, the journey towards refined M&E gains momentum.

c) Involving Beneficiaries and Communities:

The inclusion of beneficiaries and communities in M&E weaves a tapestry of ownership and accountability. Partnering with these stakeholders in data collection, analysis, and interpretation elevates the authenticity of the evaluation, ensuring that it truly encapsulates their voices and needs.

3. Using Technology: Pioneering The Digital Frontier

"Using Technology" emerges as the third strategic vista, unveiling a world of technological wonders that revolutionise M&E. Technological tools and platforms streamline processes, shattering resource and time constraints, and propelling nonprofits towards efficient M&E practices.

Delving into the Digital Landscape:

a) Data Collection Tools:

Embracing mobile data collection tools, such as smartphones or tablets, simplifies the data gathering process. Real-time data entry, error reduction, and seamless data synchronisation, even in remote settings, become the hallmarks of progress.

b) Data Management Systems:

Robust data management systems, like cloud-based databases or information management software, become the fortress that safeguards data. They ensure organised storage, easy retrieval, and secure sharing, both within the organisation and with external partners.

c) Data Visualization and Reporting Tools:

The advent of data visualisation tools and reporting software paints intricate data with a brush of simplicity. Infographics, dashboards, and interactive visualisations metamorphose complex data into accessible, engaging stories, making it comprehensible for diverse audiences.

4. Being Flexible: The Art Of Adaptive Resilience

Our fourth strategic landscape, "Being Flexible," champions the essence of adaptability. In the dynamic world of M&E, embracing change and nurturing an adaptable mindset enable nonprofits to surmount unforeseen challenges, learning from every step of the journey.

Unpacking the Essence of Flexibility:

a) Adaptive Monitoring and Evaluation:

By weaving the fabric of adaptive M&E approaches, nonprofits infuse iterative learning into their program lifecycle. Regular reviews, revisions of indicators, and a fluid evaluation plan ensure responsiveness to evolving program needs.

b) Participatory Evaluation:

Inviting program staff, beneficiaries, and stakeholders into the evaluation process kindles a culture of collaborative learning. Engaging in joint reflection, sense-making, and decision-making births a fertile ground for growth and improvement.

c) *Continuous Learning and Improvement:*

Nurturing a culture of perpetual learning and refinement amplifies the resonance of M&E. Nonprofits become adept at interpreting findings, gleaning lessons, and infusing evidence-based changes into their program design and implementation.

As we conclude this strategic voyage, the tapestry of innovative approaches to overcoming M&E challenges emerges vividly. By kindling internal capacity, fostering external partnerships, embracing technology, and nurturing adaptability, nonprofits stand poised at the threshold of transformation.

These strategic manoeuvres enhance credibility, magnify effectiveness, and amplify the impact of nonprofit programs. The culmination of these efforts extends beyond organizational growth; it becomes a beacon of positive change that radiates throughout the communities these nonprofits serve.

CHAPTER 6:

Using Monitoring and Evaluation to Improve Nonprofit Programs

W elcome to Chapter 6 of our comprehensive Book on "Strategic Nonprofits: Empowering Change through Monitoring & Evaluation." In this chapter, we will embark on a detailed exploration of how monitoring and evaluation can serve as potent instruments for enhancing nonprofit programs.

Beyond their role in shedding light on program performance, monitoring and evaluation processes have the capacity to serve as catalysts for identifying areas of enhancement, facilitating informed adjustments, and quantifying the impact of interventions.

Through adept utilization of monitoring and evaluation insights, nonprofit organizations can elevate their program outcomes and achieve a more profound social impact.

Tracking Progress: A Foundation For Effective Program Management

In the intricate landscape of program management, tracking

progress stands as an indispensable foundation. By systematically monitoring program activities, outputs, and outcomes, nonprofits can obtain an all-encompassing comprehension of their program's performance.

Defining Key Performance Indicators:

Central to effective monitoring is the identification and definition of pertinent and measurable key performance indicators (KPIs). These indicators should seamlessly align with the program's objectives and encapsulate both the qualitative and quantitative dimensions of program outcomes.

Data Collection and Analysis:

The bedrock of reliable insights lies in the implementation of robust data collection methods and systems. These methods may entail surveys, interviews, focus groups, observations, or the judicious use of existing data sources. Upon data collection, a rigorous analysis, employing fitting statistical or qualitative techniques, breathes life into the collected information, unfurling a panorama of program progress.

Regular Reporting:

The rhythm of regular reporting orchestrates a symphony of transparency and accountability. By keeping stakeholders apprised of progress and achievements, nonprofits foster a culture of openness and involvement. Crafting concise, visually engaging, and accessible reports ensures that the narrative of program progress resonates with diverse audiences.

Identifying Areas For Improvement: A Precursor To Growth

Embracing growth entails acknowledging program strengths and weaknesses. Through discerning analysis, nonprofits can pinpoint areas for improvement, setting the stage for impactful transformations.

Data Analysis and Interpretation:

In the labyrinth of data lie valuable patterns and trends. The art of data interpretation involves viewing this information through kaleidoscopic lenses, considering diverse perspectives, and mining potential areas for growth within the findings.

Engaging Stakeholders:

The resonance of monitoring and evaluation findings amplifies when stakeholders' voices chime in. Engaging beneficiaries, staff, and partners in the interpretation of findings crafts a multifaceted narrative of program challenges, germinating seeds of innovative solutions.

Conducting Root Cause Analysis:

Digging to the roots is a strategic pursuit. Root cause analysis, a systematic approach, unveils the underlying causes of bottlenecks or challenges. By dissecting these causes, nonprofits arm themselves with targeted strategies to overcome obstacles and bolster program efficiency.

Making Changes: A Symphony Of Strategic Implementation

With areas for improvement mapped, nonprofits embark on a journey of orchestrated change. This movement requires meticulous planning, agile implementation, and vigilant monitoring.

Developing Action Plans:

Blueprints for change come to life through action plans. These plans lay out a roadmap, delineating activities, responsible parties, timelines, and envisioned outcomes. This orchestration ensures that changes materialize systematically and with precision.

Piloting and Testing:

Change incubates within the crucible of piloting and testing. This phase facilitates a controlled assessment of the proposed changes on a smaller scale before full-scale deployment. By embracing this experimental phase, nonprofits mitigate risks and unleash evidence-based, impactful alterations.

Iterative Learning and Adaptation:

Change is a journey, not a destination. As changes ripple

through program landscapes, continuous monitoring ensures their efficacy. A culture of iterative learning allows nonprofits to course-correct, ensuring that program enhancement is an ongoing, ever-evolving process.

Measuring Impact: The Metamorphosis Of Outcomes

Program metamorphosis culminates in measuring impact, a crucial juncture in program evaluation.

Impact Evaluation Methods:

Unlocking the true impact necessitates sophisticated evaluation methods. Randomized controlled trials, quasi-experimental designs, and comparative case studies enable nonprofits to discern the causal threads linking their programs to observable outcomes. The result? A robust tapestry of credible evidence.

Cost-Effectiveness Analysis:

The calculus of impact extends to cost-effectiveness analysis. By weighing benefits against investments, nonprofits navigate a realm of efficiency, poised to channel resources judiciously and amplify their impact.

Utilizing Evaluation Results:

Findings gleaned from impact evaluations furnish a wealth of insights, primed to steer strategic decisions, galvanize programmatic recalibration, and illuminate resource allocation choices. Effective communication and dissemination of these results to stakeholders arm nonprofits with a catalyst for replication, scaling, or policy advocacy.

Monitoring And Evaluation: Architects Of Program Improvement

Within the realm of nonprofit programs, monitoring and evaluation don the mantle of architects of improvement. Through vigilant progress tracking, incisive identification of growth areas, strategic changes, and rigorous impact quantification, nonprofits are poised for an evolution that transcends status quo.

Utilizing Robust Methodologies:

Robust methodologies underpin the journey. Be it KPI definition, data analysis, or impact evaluation, nonprofits harness the arsenal of methodologies to wield insights with precision.

Engaging Stakeholders:

The tableau of improvement shines bright with the involvement of stakeholders. Their collective wisdom, infused through interpretation and collaboration, amplifies the trajectory of growth.

Evidence-Based Decision-Making:

At the heart of it all lies evidence. Evidence-based decisions carry the power to usher in lasting change, transforming nonprofits into dynamic agents of impactful societal transformation.

In this chapter, we traversed the landscape where monitoring and evaluation orchestrate metamorphosis. By mastering the art of tracking progress, identifying improvement avenues, orchestrating changes, and quantifying impact, nonprofits chart a trajectory of purposeful evolution.

Embracing robust methodologies, enlisting stakeholder voices, and advocating evidence-based transformation, nonprofits sow the seeds of profound social change, reaping a harvest of meaningful outcomes for the communities they serve.

CHAPTER 7:

Using Monitoring and Evaluation to Improve Nonprofit Accountability

W elcome to Chapter 7 of our comprehensive Book on "Strategic Nonprofits: Empowering Change through Monitoring & Evaluation." In this chapter, we will embark on an exploration of how monitoring and evaluation (M&E) can elevate nonprofit accountability.

Accountability stands as a vital pillar of nonprofit endeavours, serving as a beacon for transparency, a testament to impact, a builder of trust with stakeholders, and a magnet for funding. By harnessing the potency of M&E processes, nonprofits can fortify their accountability practices and unfurl a vivid banner of dedication towards achieving impactful outcomes. Let's embark on an enlightening journey through each dimension.

Unveiling Impact: A Keystone Of Accountability

Unveiling the impact of nonprofit programs is akin to illuminating the path of accountability. Nonprofits are entrusted with the mission of showcasing tangible improvements in the lives of individuals and communities they serve.

Measuring Outcomes:

The crux lies in measuring outcomes. By adopting outcome measurement frameworks and indicators, nonprofits can unfurl a tapestry of long-term changes stemming from their programs. This entails a comprehensive assessment of intended outcomes, juxtaposed against the realized results—a vivid testimony of impact and accountability.

Guiding with Baselines and Benchmarks:

The journey commences with baselines and benchmarks. Setting these at the program's inception serves as a navigational tool for gauging progress and evaluating performance against predefined standards. This yardstick paints a vivid picture of impact, assuring stakeholders of the path traversed and the destination reached.

Narrating through Real-life Tales:

The canvas of accountability springs to life through real-life narratives. Anchoring impact with real-world examples and case studies stitches an intricate tapestry of change. As nonprofits share success stories, testimonials, and qualitative accounts, they weave an unassailable narrative of the tangible transformations their interventions herald.

Trust: The Bedrock Of Accountability

Trust is the currency of accountability, underpinning every endeavour of nonprofits. Building and nurturing trust with stakeholders—including beneficiaries, donors, partners, and the broader community—forms the very bedrock of accountability.

Transparent Communication:

Transparency begets trust. Nonprofits can forge trust by fostering transparent communication. Sharing monitoring and evaluation findings, progress updates, and program reports with stakeholders illuminates the inner workings of programs, painting a clear picture of activities, outcomes, and challenges.

Engaging the Stakeholder Tapestry:

Accountability blooms through stakeholder engagement. Beneficiaries, donors, and community members become partners in the accountability dance. Their involvement in decision-making, data collection, and evaluation activities casts a resplendent spotlight on inclusivity and accountability.

The Emissary of External Validation:

External validation seals the pact of trust. Seeking independent evaluations, third-party audits, or external reviews lends an aura of credibility to nonprofit assertions. Objective assessments provide an unblemished perspective on program efficacy, fostering a sense of trust and accountability.

The Siren Song Of Funding: A Melody Of Accountability

Funding forms the lifeblood of nonprofit endeavours, sustaining operations and amplifying impact. Monitoring and evaluation, with their clarion call of accountability, play a symphonic role in wooing funders.

Narrating to Donors:

Nonprofits don the mantle of storytellers to their donors. By furnishing comprehensive and precise reports, nonprofits illuminate the path of fund utilization and achieved impact. Weaving monitoring and evaluation insights into these reports lends an air of accountability and bolsters donor confidence.

Cost-effective Serenades:

Monitoring and evaluation carry the banner of cost-effectiveness. The tale they tell is one of interventions achieving desired outcomes without breaking the bank. This siren song resonates with donors in search of impactful and efficient investments.

Harmony in Partnerships:

In harmonious partnerships lies funding's promise. Collaboration with fellow nonprofits, government agencies, or corporate allies enriches funding prospects. Through strategic alliances, nonprofits tap into a wellspring of resources, expertise, and funding opportunities—a harmonious symphony of accountability and sustainability.

Monitoring And Evaluation: The Symphony Of Accountability

Monitoring and evaluation, in unison, orchestrate a symphony of accountability for nonprofits. Through the prism of impact demonstration, trust building, and funding allure, nonprofits set a stage where transparency, outcomes, and resource stewardship are in the spotlight.

Real-life Epics and Transparent Dialogues:

Real-life narratives and transparent communication form the stars of this symphony. By sharing success stories, painting a vivid picture of activities, and candidly acknowledging challenges, nonprofits compose a harmonious tune of accountability.

The Path Forward: In the Footsteps of Accountability:

As we conclude this chapter, the footprint of accountability emerges as a legacy of monitoring and evaluation. By embracing accountability, nonprofits illuminate their path, forging connections with stakeholders, and paving the way for a symphony of meaningful social change.

In this chapter, we embarked on a journey to unravel how monitoring and evaluation (M&E) weave a tapestry of accountability for nonprofits. Through the prism of impact demonstration, trust-building, and funding attraction, nonprofits are poised to ascend the stairway of accountability, crafting a narrative steeped in transparency, outcomes, and responsible resource management—a melody resonating with profound social impact and transformation.

CHAPTER 8:

Conclusion: The Importance of Strategic Nonprofits: Empowering Change through Monitoring & Evaluation

A s we draw the curtains on this comprehensive Book, titled "Strategic Nonprofits: Empowering Change through Monitoring & Evaluation," it becomes paramount to highlight the pivotal role that monitoring, and evaluation (M&E) play within the nonprofit sector.

In this final chapter, we are set to underscore the significance of monitoring and evaluation as a cornerstone tool for nonprofits. By engaging in monitoring and evaluation processes, nonprofits have the opportunity to refine their programmes, magnify their impact, and uphold their commitment to stakeholders. Let us delve into these essential facets in greater detail.

Monitoring And Evaluation: An Indispensable Toolkit For Nonprofits

Unravelling the Essence of Monitoring:

Monitoring takes the form of a systematic journey encompassing the perpetual collection, analysis, and interpretation of data. It provides a steady compass, enabling the tracking of a programme's progress or intervention. The timely insights garnered from monitoring reveal the programme's path, pinpointing bottlenecks, unveiling challenges, and certifying that the programme remains aligned with its intended outcomes.

Magnifying the Significance of Evaluation:

Evaluation, on the other hand, expands the narrative beyond monitoring's boundaries. It homes in on a profound assessment of a programme's effectiveness, efficiency, and relevance. This rigorous scrutiny traverses the landscape of a programme's outcomes and impacts, providing a compass of evidence to discern whether the coveted transformations have indeed transpired, and attributing these transformations to the programme's strategic endeavours.

Refining Programmes Through The Prism Of Monitoring And Evaluation

Crafting a Tapestry of Program Effectiveness:

Monitoring and evaluation become the artisans of programme enhancement. By weaving the threads of systematic data collection and analysis, nonprofits acquire insights into the inner workings of their programmes.

This illumination guides decisions, unveiling successful

approaches and avenues where refinement is required. The intricate dance of data empowers nonprofits to sculpt their programme's design, execution, and resource allocation.

Efficiency as an Art Form:

The stage of regular monitoring and evaluation unfurls a tableau where inefficiencies are spotlighted. This spotlight illuminates any redundant steps or inefficiencies within programme activities.

The symphony of information resonates empowerment, granting nonprofits the capacity to streamline procedures, shed superfluous layers, and harness resources optimally. This harmonious choreography leads to financial frugality and an amplified return on investments.

The Artistry of Accountability:

Monitoring and evaluation act as the maestros composing an aria of accountability. By adorning their programmes with the jewels of tracked outcomes and transparent reports, nonprofits offer a window into their impact. This showcase of integrity, unveiled through data and narratives, fosters trust among donors, beneficiaries, partners, and the broader community—a symphony of trust that harmonizes the stakeholder ensemble.

Unleashing Impact Through Monitoring And Evaluation

The Canvas of Decision-Making:

The portals of monitoring and evaluation engender a canvas upon which decisions are painted with the hues of evidence. Nonprofits wield this evidence to shape their strategies, tailoring interventions to address emergent needs. The canvas of evidence-based decision-making ensures resources are judiciously allocated, amplifying the resonance of success.

Knowledge as a Shared Symphony:

Monitoring and evaluation cultivate a culture of learning within nonprofits. Methodically collecting and dissecting data grants organizations the privilege of gleaning lessons and embracing best practices. The orchestra of knowledge-sharing, both within and beyond the organization's walls, harmonizes nonprofits with the sector's larger chorus, nurturing innovation, and growth.

An Overture of Perpetual Refinement:

Monitoring and evaluation, when performed in synchrony, erect a bridge to continuous enhancement. The rhythms of feedback loops and insights derived from data fuel an unending journey of programme refinement. Nonprofits listen to the cadence of data, addressing limitations, honing strategies, and finetuning their interventions.

This symphony of continuous refinement ensures nonprofits stand as responsive stewards of their beneficiaries and communities.

In summation, monitoring and evaluation constitute the warp and weft of nonprofit existence. They bestow nonprofits with the tools to perfect their programmes, intensify their impact, and hold themselves in the embrace of accountability.

By embracing the dance of monitoring and evaluation, nonprofits ascend the stairway to programme excellence, orchestrating a harmonious ensemble of effectiveness, efficiency, and resonance with stakeholder expectations.

These practices etch a sonnet of evidence-based decisions, knowledge-sharing, and perpetual refinement—a sonnet that resonates as nonprofits march steadfastly towards a tapestry of meaningful transformation within the communities they serve.

CHAPTER 9:

Call to Action: Start Conducting Monitoring and Evaluation Today!

Congratulations on reaching the final chapter of our comprehensive book, "Strategic Nonprofits: Empowering Change through Monitoring & Evaluation." This chapter aims to underline the significance of taking action and commencing the journey of conducting monitoring and evaluation for your nonprofit organization.

By embracing monitoring and evaluation practices, you can enhance the efficiency, effectiveness, and impact of your programmes. Let's delve into the steps you can take to embark on this transformative voyage.

Recognizing The Value Of Monitoring And Evaluation:

Monitoring and evaluation transcend being mere bureaucratic obligations; they emerge as invaluable tools in the arsenal of nonprofit leaders. These tools facilitate informed decision-making, elevate programme outcomes, and illuminate accountability pathways to stakeholders.

Through the prism of monitoring and evaluation, you can:

- Identify strengths and areas for improvement within your programme's design and execution.
- Amplify programme effectiveness by adapting strategies grounded in evidence and feedback.
- Align your organization's endeavours with its mission and objectives.
- Communicate your programme's impact to donors, beneficiaries, and other stakeholders.
- Optimize resource allocation, ensuring judicious usage of limited resources.

Accessing Resources And Expertise:

To initiate the journey of monitoring and evaluation, tapping into a trove of resources and expertise is pivotal. Consider the following avenues:

a. Books, Articles, and Online Courses:

A plethora of books, articles, and online courses stands ready to furnish comprehensive guidance on monitoring and evaluation. These resources traverse diverse topics, encompassing evaluation frameworks, data collection techniques, analysis methodologies, and reporting best practices.

Some recommended resources include:

- 7 steps for setting up a Monitoring & Evaluation system. (https://www.activityinfo.org/blog/posts/2022-01-06-seven-steps-for-setting-up-a-monitoring-and-evaluation-system.html)

- Guidance Note 1.2: Monitoring and Reporting. (https://www.ilo.org/wcmsp5/groups/public/---ed_mas/---eval/documents/publication/wcms_746706.pdf)

- Basic principles of monitoring and evaluation. (https://www.ilo.org/wcmsp5/groups/public/---ed_emp/documents/publication/wcms_546505.pdf)

b. Engaging Monitoring and Evaluation Professionals:

In instances of overwhelm or internal capacity limitations, forging partnerships with monitoring and evaluation professionals emerges as a prudent step.

These experts offer bespoke guidance, formulate evaluation blueprints, aid in data collection and analysis, and proffer insights to refine your nonprofit's monitoring and evaluation practices.

When seeking professionals, prioritise those with a proven track record in the nonprofit sector and a robust comprehension of evaluation methodologies.

Designing And Implementing An M&E Plan:

To effectively venture into monitoring and evaluation, the construction of a meticulously designed M&E plan tailored to your nonprofit's distinctive requirements becomes paramount. Delve into the following facets:

a. Clear Objectives and Indicators:

Sketch out the purpose and objectives of your monitoring and evaluation endeavours. Erect measurable indicators that harmonise with your programme's objectives, facilitating the monitoring of progress and the evaluation of impact.

b. Data Collection Methods:

Navigate the seas of suitable data collection methods, aligning them with your programme's context and resources. This nautical journey may encompass surveys, interviews, focus groups, observations, or the analysis of existing data.

c. Data Analysis and Interpretation:

Contemplate the compass guiding the analysis and interpretation of the amassed data. Choose suitable analytical tools and techniques to extract resonant insights, unveiling trends and patterns that tell tales of significance.

d. Reporting and Utilisation of Findings:

Craft a blueprint for disseminating evaluation findings to stakeholders—donors, board members, staff, and beneficiaries. Ensuring that these findings are conveyed in a lucid, succinct, and actionable manner is paramount. Harness the fruits of these results to steer decision-making, refine programme strategies, and narrate the impact of your nonprofit's noble work.

Conclusion:

By initiating action and unfurling the canvas of monitoring and evaluation, you're steering your nonprofit toward the shores of perpetual improvement. This journey amplifies transparency, magnifies impact, and hones accountability. As you traverse these waters, remember that each step taken brings you closer to a realm of efficacy, influence, and honourable stewardship of the communities you serve.

ACKNOWLEDGEMENT

I wish to convey my profound appreciation to all those who have provided unwavering support and inspiration throughout the incredible journey of crafting this book.

Foremost, my heartfelt gratitude goes to my beloved mother, Alhaja Sherifat Somotun, and my siblings, whose unwavering love and encouragement have been my pillars of strength. Their belief in both me and my work has been an unwavering source of motivation.

To my mentors, Dr Olugbenga Asaolu and Dr Oladipupo Banji Ipadeola, I extend my sincere thanks for your invaluable guidance and uplifting encouragement. Your wealth of wisdom and seasoned experience have been indispensable in helping me navigate the intricate challenges encountered during the creation of this book.

My gratitude also extends to my former colleagues at Malaria Consortium Nigeria, Association for Reproductive and Family Health, and Society for Family Health. Your steadfast support and camaraderie have warmed my heart and buoyed my spirits.

A special note of appreciation is reserved for my former boss, Dr John Dada, whose insightful guidance, and unwavering support have significantly shaped my professional journey. His leadership and mentorship have been a cornerstone of my growth.

Lastly, to each and every reader who has taken the time to delve into these pages, I offer my heartfelt thanks. Your embrace of this book fills me with gratitude beyond words, and I am truly humbled by your support.

With the utmost sincerity and deepest gratitude,

Olasheni Somotun, MPH.

ABOUT THE AUTHOR

Olasheni Somotun

Olasheni Somotun, MPH, is a results-driven public health expert, holding a Master of Public Health (MPH) degree in Health Policy and Management from the esteemed University of Ibadan, Nigeria. He also holds a bachelor's degree in microbiology from Olabisi Onabanjo University.

With an impressive eight-year track record of expertise in monitoring and evaluation (M&E) within the dynamic realm of public health, Somotun has emerged as a catalyst for significant transformation in community health implementation. Serving as a Senior Monitoring & Evaluation Officer at Malaria Consortium in Niger State, Nigeria, he played a pivotal role in the successful management and conclusion of the $2 million BMGF Technical Assistance Project for Community Health Implementation Promoters and Services (CHIPS) initiative.

Olasheni's proficiency in database management and focused capacity building has empowered community-based organizations (CBOs) to excel in the demanding USAID Site Improvement Monitoring System (SIMS). His versatility extends to a range of roles, including that of Monitoring and Evaluation Research Consultant for Global Fund Malaria and HIV/AIDS, as well as an Intern/Volunteer at the ESMPIN Project.

In addition to being a proficient team player and adept communicator, Olasheni has effectively engaged with stakeholders at both national and state government levels and development partners. This engagement has fostered robust partnerships and coordination, laying the groundwork for efficient programme execution.

Fuelled by an unyielding commitment to continuous learning, Olasheni has obtained additional certifications in Google Project Management, Google Data Analytics, Monitoring, Evaluation, Accountability, and Learning (MEAL), as well as various other pertinent domains.

Beyond his noteworthy professional accomplishments, Olasheni is a devoted family man, fluent in both English and Yoruba. He is steadfastly dedicated to unlocking the full potential of monitoring and evaluation, propelling public health initiatives to unprecedented heights of accomplishment.

You can connect with Olasheni on his professional LinkedIn page (linkedin.com/in/olasheni-a-somotun-mph-97776335) and embark on a transformative voyage that redefines the boundaries of monitoring and evaluation, as you jointly pursue impactful change.

Made in the USA
Middletown, DE
22 September 2023

38990281R00035